SNOW FALLING ON SNOW

Copyright: © 2015 Renée Gregorio
Paperback ISBN: 978-1-941783-03-0

All rights reserved: except for the purpose of quoting brief passages for review, no part of this book may be reproduced or transmitted in any form or by any means, electronic or mechanical, including photocopying, recording, or by any information storage and retrieval system, without permission in writing from the publisher.

Cover art and ink drawings: John Brandi
Back cover art: Royce Hamel
Author Photo: Kara Duval
Cover & interior design/layout: Steven Asmussen
Copyediting: Elizabeth Nichols

Glass Lyre Press, LLC.
P.O. Box 2693
Glenview, IL 60026

www.GlassLyrePress.com

Snow Falling on Snow

Poems By
Renée Gregorio

for Nancy Shanteau

Preface

Several years ago I began a morning practice of writing tanka. I've worked in the form and liked it for a long time, for its brevity and sharpness and the ways in which it encourages clarity of thought, feeling, and image. During this practice, I wrote several tanka each morning, focusing first on whatever was happening outside myself, in nature, in the neighborhood, in the garden. What were the sounds, sights, sensations, scents occurring all around me? I then turned inward, asking: how does what's external interact with what's internal? What is the unusual thread, the shadow, the spark that is created by the interaction between these realities?

Thus the writing of morning tanka as a means of beginning my day became established, an awareness practice that gave me a particular kind of awakening to the world around me and within me. This set a different mood and way of seeing in my life. Akin to meditation, the writing of tanka settled something in me and opened doorways to the unseen. It brought alive the everyday that surrounded me; much like turning a key in a lock, it opened doors to perception that were previously shut.

I stepped into my days with the knowledge that I had taken time to see and feel my place in the world before entering it. And the practice was transportable. I wrote tanka at home in El Rito, New Mexico, at my place in Santa Fe, and while traveling in other countries. Sometimes notes from travel turned into tanka when I returned home. After two years of this practice, I'd written hundreds of tanka, which I then revised and revised some more, then cut up the poems and pinned each to a board to grasp the right order for what eventually became *Snow Falling on Snow*.

Tanka writing helps me hone in on what is essential, and this sharpens all my writing, my relationships, my work — my life. This morning I read one of Shodo Harada Sensei's Zen insights, in which he states: "When we see, we see with our whole body. When we hear, our entire body is our ear." He talks about how our mental understanding creates a gap between the seer and the seen. He says that when nothing is inserted here, when there is no gap, we can know the "actuality of life's energy." This is what tanka practice is to me: a place on the page to begin to understand life without a gap between subject and object.

I call these poems "tanka," keeping in mind the spirit of the form and the reformation that exists within its lineage. Many have brought their own social context, place, and language to bear on the Japanese form, and such commerce between cultures has changed it over time. I enjoy the beat and pulse of language as I count syllables that add up to the 5-7-5-7-7 or 31-syllable count. Although I don't strictly adhere to this, I like the rigorous dance it invites with language. This engagement is much like another practice I have, which is to perform a *kata* with the *jo* — a staff used in the martial art aikido that embraces 31 counts or moves.

Tanka has evolved through several movements that shifted it in form and subject matter. Once Western literature's effect blended with the Japanese poetic sensibility, even more reform came, which led to the modern tanka. Of the several reform movements, I most identify with the *shasei* movement, which originated with the work of Masaoka Shiki in the nineteenth century. *Shasei* was then interpreted as an external, visual "sketch from life". The next evolution occurred under the Araragi group in the early part of the twentieth century, especially with the work of Saito Mokichi, who expanded *shasei* to include psychic and biological observations. He brought in the idea of life energy or force, much as Harada Sensei's insights do, saying that *shasei* is really a union of nature and the self, or the external and the internal. This merging happens in the tanka, where if we are lucky, the perceiver and what's perceived come together, and we can begin to sense this quality of oneness.

—Renée Gregorio
El Rito, New Mexico
August 2014

Contents

Snow Falling on Snow	15
Mud on the Mats	35
A River in the Body	43
Bird Nest in a Hat	61
Acknowledgments	77
About the Author	79

Snow Falling on Snow

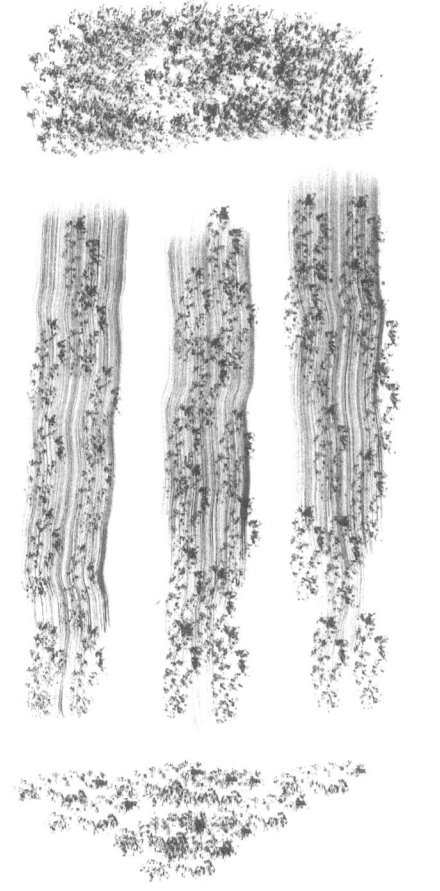

snow dust forms crystals
in ten degree morning
I gather laundry
circumambulate the past
make an extra cup of coffee

                                        in the stillness
                                        three things become visible—
                                        the caldera
                                        Pedernal and the empty field—
                                        all made clearer by what's absent

each morning there's time
to wake up, cultivate silence
find the river
within these words
this current of breath

                                          water steams atop
                                          woodstove's bright red heat
                                          yesterday's snow
                                          slides off the metal porch chairs—
                                          inside and out, burning

the home fire's steady
wood burns from kindling to ash
such a brief journey
smoke curls from neighbors' stovepipes
we're all warmed by the same wood

                                        snow falls all night long
                                        he lights the fire before I rise
                                        in the darkened room
                                        the cold air of night lingers
                                        I stand with my back to the flames

old lover's blue eyes
I dream them in another's face
asking, asking
for something unnamable—
what request unlocks the door?

                        there's a thread that runs
                        between the graves of ex-lovers
                        among the living—
                        of this world, out of this world
                        I walk with them all

house of soft light
absorbed by pale yellow walls
a friend speaks what's true
the heart inside me grows large
as mountains turn to blood

say the word *river*
even if its bed is dry
mountains hold the snow
give a name to what's unseen
and water finds its course

grey cloud cover
chopping block on trampled snow
I raise the axe—
the blade releases the wood
into two perfect halves

one lamp burns strongest
in this house I name mine
what's inside blossoms
when outside is coldest
we're deep into winter now

books weighty on their shelves—
not enough space, they tumble down
give me solitude
a place without thought
the sound of snow falling on snow

                                        I empty trash
                                        move papers from bags to desk
                                        pile to pile
                                        go outside to split more wood
                                        there's grace when the snow begins

awake too much
when I'm supposed to be sleeping
don't tell me who to see
or when to see them!—my boat
ready to be launched: push off!

                                              a woman carries
                                              the candle and the flame
                                              lets wax drip
                                              hot onto her clutched hand
                                              she keeps holding the light

digital clock:
3:00, 4:00, then 5:00 am
sleep remedies useless
I read poems about death
listen to songs about wildflowers

                                    wore a fedora
                                    Pharoah's bass player said "Hi!
                                    you look good." He played Coltrane
                                    through gold silk shirt, shock of gray hair
                                    my white transparent dress

I desire movement
not ice or this frozen ground
there's still far to go
beyond roads packed hard with snow
recalling everyone I've loved

what might have been snow
shifts to night rain
time to drive home
on roads clear of ice
led all the way by my heart

grey desert sky
huge raven on the post
fence lined with snow
I am hungry for the river
the ways in which your hands meet mine

                                          threat of snow
                                          inside, what can be imagined?
                                          downy softness
                                          cold growing on windowpanes
                                          the candle I will light

all these days indoors
forgetting the breadth of sky
how stars occupy space
if I look up they're still there
shining because of the dark

                    in the dusky room
                    dreams of stepping forward
                    all my relatives
                    surround me clapping their hands—
                    when will applause come from within?

winter solitude
scratch of pen on paper
a robin outside
plants her feet on snowdrift
her beak pokes frozen ground

                                          I dream my teacher
                                          gives me an envelope bursting
                                          with money, tells me
                                          to have no other. All night
                                          snow falls on the snowy ground

my friend tells me
her dying mother comes and goes
yesterday she asked:
tell me, how many people
were there at my funeral?

                                            she lies beside
                                            her mother as she wanes
                                            moves in and out
                                            of luminosity
                                            the veil between worlds, so thin

so disappointed
this early morning—the promised
snowfall already turning
to ice on the pine bough
as my heart clings to old love

                          I read old postcards
                          fifteen years that man's been dead
                          what can I still hear?
                          his footfall on each threshold
                          his brush meeting the blank canvas

I clean cobwebs
from *vigas* and dark corners
happy in solitude
I saw the moon rise full at dawn
felt my heart slip into place

                        heavy clouds, some snow
                        six black cows feasting in the field
                        music's playing:
                        just give me one thing that I can hold
                        onto: the jade plant's new green

Mud on the Mats

on the mats I practice
what I know and what I don't
how fierceness and love
occupy this space between us—
where our swords touch, we shine

swept pale green mats
the altar's bird of paradise
hen, change. *ka*, form.
I hope for fluidity
desire dialogue

aikido bruises—
red welt on left wrist, thigh darkened
it makes me happy
this place of body and spirit's
indistinguishable whirl

                                      "bigger!" he tells me
                                      I open my chest, allow the strength
                                      of his body to enter mine
                                      turn, he's there with me
                                      throw him, he flies away

he lines us up by rank
calls for *randori's* many attacks
I take the falls
exhausted, it's my turn to throw
I can't remember their faces

                                          his shout as loud as
                                          the foghorn that leads boats
                                          away from danger
                                          his tenderness as soft
                                          as this newly fallen snow

little Bridget learns
how to wield a sword, her hands
barely wrap around it
the long form's easy to recall
but her hips— still a mystery

                                          as wide as oars
                                          and cutting as deep
                                          encouraging
                                          the heart of us to blend—
                                          sensei's hands

was that love
in the perfect landscaping
over red wine goodbyes
when I got cocky as
we counted rank at each table?

                                              her voice is shaking
                                              as she tells me she wants him
                                              I hear the flame
                                              of the water heater ignite—
                                              will her broken bone ever heal?

twenty-four grilled steaks
cooked fast in blazing flames
precisely as ordered
what is sensei leaving behind?
each table set in black and white

                        all that's clear—
                        his perfect technique
                        the moves he makes
                        behind the closed door, gossip
                        leaks through, muddies the swept mats

A River in the Body

today the wind died
and with it all smallness
there is a river
in the body—as it flows
it pushes against the banks

                                spring comes
                                on a wild horse's back
                                he bucks and whinnies
                                snow covers the driest of grounds—
                                let's dig a patch of earth

does every body
long to be discovered?
weaned on pasta
it's hard to reveal myself
I must eat less to feel more

                                    I am not what I do
                                    and I am deeply what I do
                                    if I stare at the rock
                                    in the river, the rock becomes
                                    river, becomes me, is itself

all day unpacking
I try to do it slowly
but a word is poking
at the periphery
of the unseen: *listen*

wake in a haze
dark circles ring my eyes
hair unkempt
what dreams dishevel me so?
the rug pulled out from under

the copper rose blooms
its many branches profuse
with scent and flower
too soon petals fall to the ground
I want the color to stay

                                        today we planted
                                        thirteen ponderosa pines
                                        I liked digging holes
                                        placing baby trees in earth
                                        circling each with small stones

what is it I want?
full moon's rise over low hills
unabashed shine, stars
that form one by one in this
unadulterated sky

                                        cold spring morning
                                        stream's pulse through earth and trees
                                        strong black coffee in hand
                                        in my heart, an unfurling:
                                        the iris's dark beard

what makes the dance work?
music we love, two bodies—
not only what you hear
but what we hear together—
listen hard, we'll keep spinning

                              what's left of love?
                              I do for you, you for me
                              you speak, I listen
                              there are thousands of ways to bow
                              give me your hand, I'll take it

two bright chairs
rest on the pale wooden deck
piñon spotted hills
echo back a dry beauty
fenceposts set crooked on purpose

                                      spring arrives
                                      temperature drops
                                      we wake to snow
                                      I unearth files of old writing
                                      can't remember what's fiction

wind rips through elms
through pale green pea vines
through our bodies
when will it let seeds sprout?
I yearn for the blossoming

                                       San Ildefonso Pueblo
                                       they turn toward center always
                                       shake basket and bough
                                       men and women dancing—
                                       waves, cascades, mountains

yesterday's sun, gone
season of indecision
heavy cloud cover
I want to hibernate—
but I saw the first daffodil!

                        small fire inside, clouds out
                        spring is here, then not here
                        we pluck and weed
                        tend a slowly growing garden
                        wait for the full bloom to arrive

if a bud begins
to take shape on the tree branch
then the air turns cold
does it huddle, hold its life
deep within, waiting for spring?

                                        greening hills
                                        four new purple irises
                                        ancient pine still growing
                                        we sit beneath pure aqua sky
                                        even the birds have stopped singing

wind-filled desert
hot pink apple blossoms
nearly bursting
I think of the ways of hearts
how they open despite storm

                                      wind through thick bamboo
                                      we make love indoors
                                        as sky and air clear
                                      fifteen years walking a path
                                      beside another—such heat!

the silent stream waits
a crazy screaming wind
seeps through each crack
white sills lined with fine brown sand
the fields distilled to dust

                                          today the sun rises
                                          like any other day
                                          then clouds shield it
                                          I desire the ground's warmth
                                          how it embraces the seed

this first day of spring
I want to reclaim what's lost—
breadth and vision, speech
of my blood and bones—tomorrow
I will walk to the river

                                        one orange poppy
                                        blooms among rose-bush and thorn
                                        inside its center
                                        black brushstrokes like birthmarks
                                        how it dares to be beautiful

rake away old stacks
brambles, sticks and weeds
scratch the earth's surface
churn up what's dark and rich
make new ground for tiny seeds

                                    what is true north?
                                    it's where the garden grows
                                    it's when the Milky Way
                                    takes its place in the night sky—
                                    it's the voice inside, speaking

Bird Nest in a Hat

happy to be home
I leave my feet bare all day
wash each windowsill
consider what's left undone
my hair cinched, in a tangle

veiled sunrise through clouds
last night's lightning cracked the sky
even the magpies
move quietly this morning
I wake slowly to this pen

pristine blue sky
so clear I see all the way
to Nuna's kitchen
window to the back yard
red flowers of her apron

                                I stumble in what's past
                                London streets, pubs and trains
                                fledgling work laid bare
                                to the critiques of elder writers—
                                now, the woodpecker's steady pounding

booths of hairpieces
wooden toys, *mochillas*
all made in China
everyone looks like somebody
I know back home, reborn

bamboo creaks
as the sun slowly goes down
a black cat arrives
around the back of a blue house
in the distance, mourning doves

the transvestite smiles
coyly at my husband—
body of aqua
dark neck adorned with white pearls
her tremor of voice still a man's

                                       late into night, drivers
                                       make their rickshaws into beds
                                       line the boulevard
                                       asleep, their legs askew
                                       arms thrown back as pillows

jagged spires over Leh
we cross prayer-wheel-blessed bridges
climb to Tisseru
shield our eyes to the glint—
army trucks on Tibet's border

                                      this silence
                                      echoes the quiet of home
                                      here among *chortens*
                                      the spring runs all winter—
                                      Yangchan brings us two milk coffees

on the pier
fishermen cut the flesh
of *Huauchinango*
make their catch into fillets
throw their hearts back to sea

                                         blue house, orange house
                                         hot pink shack among dirt paths
                                         the wind increases
                                         I hear the way bamboo sways
                                         her breasts over her lover's mouth

in this heat we must
saunter and nap, wake up
to saunter and nap
the little girl dressed in pink
holds her mother's pink-gloved hand

                                        Balinese wind chimes
                                        echo back to *kebaya*
                                        stiff lace of beauty
                                        wedding sarong tied too tightly
                                        hips swaying on the forest path

I read poems
of my dead teacher, ex-lover
between the lines
smell hotel rooms and sex
the way my skin holds his name

                                           one old boyfriend
                                           visits with his dark mustache
                                           another calls
                                           makes promises he can't keep
                                         I drive the long commute home

each day clouds gather
above elms and tin roof
there's no rain— I long
to dive from the highest rock
into a pool of clear water

                        in this village
                        buzz of fly, distant bird-song
                        I let the sun strike
                        my face, the bent curve of arm—
                        each cell lightens as I write

bearded iris
purple veins on white background
fluorescent yellow heart
pungent beauty of scent, the way
it shamelessly reveals its core

                                            beneath the chair
                                            a circle of leaves, the earth
                                            moistened by thunderstorms
                                            at dawn I wake to wet stones
                                            a bird nest in a hat

meadowlark, flycatcher
mourning doves—their songs circle
this square of land
what is home if not bird-cry
the tractor's huff, his breath

car tires on gravel
hummingbird's insistent chatter
sun rises fast and hot
bedcovers disheveled
wingbeat of the passing crow

the Asian rain tree
grows despite hot fiery wind
its new chartreuse branch
decides its own direction
the trunk's old wood solid

                                          morning stillness
                                        the mockingbird's liquid song
                                        is a question
                                        that forms itself in the air
                                        my heart listens for its answer

Acknowledgments

I gratefully acknowledge the following journals and publishers for the publication of these tanka:

Ribbons, Winter Issue, 2011: "today the wind died"

Moonbathing, Issue #5, 2011: "snow dust forms crystals"

Red Lights, January 2011: "pristine blue sky" and "winter solitude"

Malpais Review, Volume 3, #2, 2012: "San Ildefonso Pueblo", "heavy clouds, some snow", winter solitude", and "the home fire's steady"

Tangram, 2012: A letterpress selection of six tanka from *Snow Falling on Snow:* "snow dust forms crystals", "I am not what I do", "in this village", "spring arrives", "grey desert sky", and "bearded iris"

About the Author

Renée Gregorio's published collections of poetry include *The Skins of Possible Lives, The Storm That Tames Us, Water Shed: Aikido Tanka, Road to the Cloud's House* (with John Brandi), *Drenched,* and *Love & Death: Greatest Hits* (with Joan Logghe and Miriam Sagan). Her poetry is informed equally by the stillness and expansiveness of northern New Mexico as it is by her wide-ranging travels to places such as Bali, Thailand, Laos, Cambodia, Vietnam, Mexico, Cuba, and India. She holds a master's degree in creative writing from Antioch University, the rank of sandan in the martial art aikido, and certification as a master somatic coach. In working as a coach and teacher, she holds an integrated approach that blends her own creative experience with her work in somatics and her long-time practice of aikido. Renée helps her clients write and live from a grounded and inspired state of being as they deepen and embody their distinct expression.

INDEX

SNOW FALLING ON SNOW

snow dust forms crystals	17
in the stillness	17
each morning there's time	18
water steams atop	18
the home fire's steady	19
snow falls all night long	19
old lover's blue eyes	20
there's a thread that runs	20
house of soft light	21
say the word *river*	21
grey cloud cover	22
one lamp burns strongest	22
books weighty on their shelves—	23
I empty trash	23
awake too much	24
a woman carries	24
digital clock:	25
wore a fedora	25
I desire movement	26
what might have been snow	26
grey desert sky	27
threat of snow	27
all these days indoors	28
in the dusky room	28
winter solitude	29
I dream my teacher	29
my friend tells me	30
she lies beside	30
so disappointed	31
I read old postcards	31
I clean cobwebs	32

heavy clouds, some snow	32

Mud on the Mats

on the mats I practice	36
swept pale green mats	36
aikido bruises—	37
"bigger!" he tells me	37
he lines us up by rank	38
his shout as loud as	38
little Bridget learns	39
as wide as oars	39
was that love	40
her voice is shaking	40
twenty-four grilled steaks	41
all that's clear—	41

A River in the Body

today the wind died	45
spring comes	45
does every body	46
I am not what I do	46
all day unpacking	47
wake in a haze	47
the copper rose blooms	48
today we planted	48
what is it I want?	49
cold spring morning	49
what makes the dance work?	50
what's left of love?	50
two bright chairs	51
spring arrives	51
wind rips through elms	52
San Ildefonso Pueblo	52
yesterday's sun, gone	53
small fire inside, clouds out	53
if a bud begins	54
greening hills	54

wind-filled desert	55
wind through thick bamboo	55
the silent stream waits	56
today the sun rises	56
this first day of spring	57
one orange poppy	57
rake away old stacks	58
what is true north?	58

BIRD NEST IN A HAT

happy to be home	63
veiled sunrise through clouds	63
pristine blue sky	64
I stumble in what's past	64
booths of hairpieces	65
bamboo creaks	65
the transvestite smiles	66
late into night, drivers	66
jagged spires over Leh	67
this silence	67
on the pier	68
blue house, orange house	68
in this heat we must	69
Balinese wind chimes	69
I read poems	70
one old boyfriend	70
each day clouds gather	71
in this village	71
bearded iris	72
beneath the chair	72
meadowlark, flycatcher	73
car tires on gravel	73
the Asian rain tree	74
morning stillness	74

Glass Lyre Press

exceptional works to replenish the spirit

Glass Lyre Press is an independent literary publisher interested in technically accomplished, stylistically distinct, and original work. Glass Lyre seeks diverse writers that possess a dynamic aesthetic, and an ability to emotionally and intellectually engage a wide audience of readers.

Glass Lyre's vision is to connect the world through language and art. We hope to expand the scope of poetry and short fiction for the general reader through exceptionally well-written books, which evoke emotion, provide insight, and resonate with the human spirit.

Poetry Collections
Poetry Chapbooks
Select Short & Flash Fiction
Anthologies

www.GlassLyrePress.com

www.ingramcontent.com/pod-product-compliance
Lightning Source LLC
Chambersburg PA
CBHW060504080526
44584CB00015B/1538